cool sites

FREE STUFF
FOR KiDS
ON THE NET

By
Lisa Trumbauer

M

The Millbrook Press
Brookfield, Connecticut

Produced by 17th Street Productions,
a division of Daniel Weiss Associates, Inc.
33 West 17th Street, New York, NY 10011

Special Projects Editor, Laura Burns

Library of Congress Cataloging-in-Publication Data

Trumbauer, Lisa, 1963–
    Cool sites. Free stuff for kids on the Net / by Lisa Trumbauer.
      p.   cm.
    Summary: Describes the best websites offering items for children,
including games, posters, and manufacturer's giveaways. Contains reviews by
computer users, aged seven to twelve.
    ISBN 0-7613-1508-X (lib. bdg.). — ISBN 0-7613-1025-8 (pbk.)
    1. Children's Web sites—Directories—Juvenile literature. 2. Free
material—Computer network resourses—Directories—Juvenile literature.
[1.Web sites. 2. Free material.] I. Title. II. Title: Free stuff for kids on the Net.
ZA4226.T78   1999
025.04'083—dc21   98-49735
                                       CIP
                                       AC

pbk: 10 9 8 7 6 5 4 3 2 1
lib: 10 9 8 7 6 5 4 3 2 1

CONTENTS

GET READY TO CRUISE THE WEB!

Have you ever wanted to learn what kinds of free stuff you could find on the web? You're not alone! We asked a bunch of kids all over the country what their favorite web sites were to get and do free stuff. Many of their sites are in here. We've added others that we thought you might like too. For most of the sites all you need is your computer, an Internet provider, and your own nimble fingers as you type, point, and click your keyboard and mouse. Other sites might ask for a special tool to run games or see graphics. Each time this happens, the web site will tell you what it needs. Then you decide if you want to add the special tool to your computer files (or *download* it) or just go somewhere else.

FREEBIE FEST

You'll find that freebies come in two forms. Some freebies are free stuff you send away for and receive by mail. But most Internet freebies are things you do at a web site—for free! Like, instead of having to buy computer games or craft books or even magazines, you can find them for free on the Internet. Different web sites let you play games, or download computer stuff, or print out coloring pages, or provide instructions for craft projects, or even read books, stories, or magazines on-line—all for free! It's pretty cool! Just surf on over to the web pages listed here and you'll find hours of free fun.

WARNING!

It seems like the Internet is perfectly safe. For the most part, it is! There are, however, a few things to be careful about:

- Never give out your full name and address to a stranger or to someone you've met on the Internet.

- If a site asks you to sign up and give personal info, ask your parents first. This is a must!

- If you go into chat rooms, be careful how much you tell about yourself.

The Internet isn't scary—it's fun! But just like when you walk down a new street or ride your bike, you need to be careful. When on the web, watch where you're going, what you're doing, and who you're talking to.

Now warm up those fingers, rub your eyes clear, and get ready to explore the net!

SPECIAL NOTE

The web is a changing, growing creature that's put together by thousands of people. Sometimes a site might drop something that was there only yesterday. Other times the site has added something new and even cooler than what we first found. Sometimes the address for a web page might get totally screwy and out of whack. If you type in an address and a message tells you it can't be found, search for it using a web-search tool.

Your Internet provider probably has its own search tool; for example, America Online has Netfind. Here are some others you can hook up to:

AltaVista . . . . http://www.altavista.digital.com
Excite. . . . . http://www.excite.com
Infoseek . . . . http://www.infoseek.com
Webcrawler . . . . . . http://www.webcrawler.com
Yahoo. . . . . http://www.yahoo.com
Yahooligans
–just for kids! . . . . . http://www.yahooligans.com

GET YOUR FEET WET!

Do you want to discover all the free stuff you can find on the Internet? Get your feet wet by checking out these sites, which offer a little bit of everything!

CURiOCiTY'S FREEZONE

http://www.freezone.com

We can't say enough about this site! Sign on for ultracool, tons-of-fun stuff to do. You can send cyberpostcards to your friends and family on-line, check out what's going on in cities around the country, play games, and even learn how to set up your own web page, all for free! Plus, you can subscribe to a free E-zine, updated weekly. This site is a definite must for you cyberjunkies out there!

There's a lot to do at this site. When I was on, you could get a copy of Curiocity *magazine for free. You could also enter the Build a Small Soldier contest.*

—Tim, grade 7

GUSTOWN

http://www.gustown.com/home/gustownsummer.html

Bored? Looking for something to do? Then visit GusTown! Stop by the game gallery in the library to play one of the eight free games. Or learn how to create a new craft—the directions are free! (You can send your own craft ideas too!) Or check out the Cyberbud Kitchen in the library for a free, fun recipe. Finish a story, change the pictures on your desktop, and more—all without spending a dime!

I like the Cyberbud Theater in the Library. There are minimovies—for free.

—Pamela, grade 5

EDDY THE ECO-DOG

http://www.eddytheeco-dog.com

Ride along with Eddy the Eco-Dog as he surfs across Earth and through outer space! At this site you'll find free games and word finds, free riddles, free animal books to print out and put together, free comics to read and draw, and free pages to print and color. And oh, yeah—most of the activities give free advice for how we can take care of planet Earth. Lots of fun!

This page is a blast! There are all sorts of games and activities that tell us about Earth. In the Clubhouse part there was a free reporter guide and press badge you could print out. Very cool!

—Thomas, grade 6

BEN & JERRY'S FUN STUFF

http://euphoria.benjerry.com/fun/index.html

Here's the scoop! (Sorry—we couldn't resist!) You'll find lots of free things to keep you busy at this web page, set up by the makers of Ben & Jerry's ice cream. Besides lots of free games, like Make Ben and Jerry Hairy and The Scoop Game, you'll find free patterns and instructions for making lots of crafts, including a bobbing-head paper cow!

There's a whole section on holiday crafts. There was a skeleton pattern you could print out, then put together. You could make the arms and legs on the skeleton move too!

—Alonso, grade 5

COLGATE KIDS WORLD

http://www.colgate.com/Kids-world

Okay, so this is a little hokey. But there's lots of free stuff to do here. Upon entering Dr. Rabbit's No Cavities Clubhouse, you can play connect the dots for free, print out a free toothbrush chart, freely explore the jungle game for healthy snacks, and print out free coloring pages.

THE IRWIN FUN FACTORY

http://www.irwin-toy.com

If you surf on over to this site, you'll find some neat free stuff. You can adopt a virtual cyberpet for free (if you are under 12, you have to get your parents' permission), play a free game of Slide-O sliding tiles, or check out the free coloring pages for the English cartoon characters Wallace and Gromit. Once you enter the Fun Factory, click Fun and Games to find all the free stuff!

HORSEFUN

http://www.horsefun.com

Are you into horses? Then you've got to check into this web site! You'll find lots of free stuff about horses, like free puzzles to solve, a free story to read, a free contest to enter, and free facts about horses. So saddle up and ride on by!

I love horses, so this is one of my favorite sites. You can enter a coloring contest to win a blue satin first-place ribbon. You have to send your entry to Australia, but that's kind of cool too!

—Vickie, grade 6

3-2-1 . . . DOWNLOAD!

From games to screen savers to animation and minimovies, there's a ton of stuff you can download and keep on your computer. And all the downloads at these web sites are free!

MiCROSOFT KiDS!

http://www.microsoft.com/kids/freestuff

Yes, this computer supergiant has a web page (of course!) with a section just for kids. You'll find lots of games to download. But more importantly, this is one of the sites that allows you to download—*for free!*—the software Shockwave. As you surf the web you'll find that you need Shockwave to run many of the games and other on-line stuff. This site is a must-visit!

This site is a little too young for me, but it has some fun games. And it's great that you can get Shockwave.

—Patricia, grade 9

EDMARK

http://www.edmark.com/free

This educational company has a few free downloads, with a chance to get more! If you download your free copy of Jungle Chess, you'll be enrolled to win the monthly drawing of Strategy Challenges, Collections 1 and 2. And if you download their free electronic geoboard, you'll be enrolled to win the monthly drawing of Mighty Math. There's other stuff going on here too, so stop by!

FAMILY GAMES

http://www.familygames.com/free/freegame.html

You'll find lots of free games to download here. A colorful menu gives you a tiny sample of each game, like Oktagon, Valvo, and Hierophant. Go to the bottom of the page and click Shareware to find more downloadable games, all with an educational twist, like Spell-Mell and Twisted Tails.

DK KiDS DiNo FUN

http://www.dkonline.com/preview

DK is short for Dorling Kindersley—a children's book publisher. Click on Goodies. You'll see tons of stuff to download for free, with a dinosaur theme, of course! There are free door hangers, invitations, labels, postcards, wallpaper, envelopes, and, of course, instructions that explain how to download.

The dinosaur stationery is the best! There's one with the dinosaur practically tearing through the paper. I downloaded the pages to use to write letters.

—Stacey, grade 5

QUESTACON KiDSPACE

http://sunsite.anu.edu.au/Questacon/ks_main.html

One of the coolest things about this site from Australia is that you can download minidinosaur movies! Click "See Questacon's robotic dinosaurs." Choose your dinosaur, like *T. rex, Apatosaurus,* or *Stegosaurus,* then choose your computer capability. You'll find other free stuff at this site too, like coloring pages and games.

This page is good if you like dinosaurs. You'll see a dinosaur that's only been discovered in Australia—Muttaburrasaurus. You can download a free minimovie of this dinosaur too!

—Lyle, grade 6

21

ALiVE SoFTWARE

http://www.alivesoft.com

From educational to "action arcade," you'll find demos for eight cool games to download for free. Animal Quest, Dinosaur Predators, and Billy the Kid Returns are just a sampling of the fun games at this site. Read the game descriptions, then choose the game you want to download. It really is that simple!

My favorite game so far (I haven't tried them all) is Snow White's Voyage. This isn't just the old fairy tale. You have to help Snow White outsmart her stepmother, the evil queen.

—Sam, grade 5

KiDS DoMAiN

http://www.kidsdomain.com

You'll find lots of free downloads here, like the Quest for the Ruby game and Mushu Numbers. You can also download clip art and all sorts of educational stuff, like Complete Toolbox, Thinking Games, and Worksheet Creations. There was even a special Magic School Bus Sand Castle Builder to download for free! It looked awesome!

I love the pictures you can download, like Dr. Seuss and goofy pictures other people sent in. Check out the gargoyles!

—Kimberly, grade 7

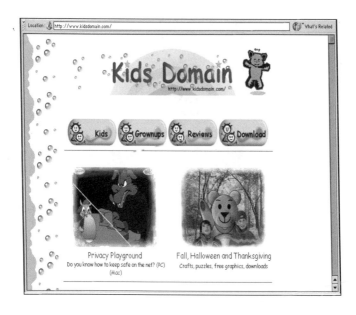

SKYLIGHT'S KIDS GRAPHICS

http://members.xoom.com/Sky_Light

Download free awesome images to jazz up your computer screen! Clip art, borders and backgrounds, cyberpets, and tile backgrounds (like wallpaper)—they're all right here for you to download, free of charge! Instructions at the site tell you how to do it too.

The borders and background designs are great! I printed them out to use as journal pages. I found lots of other pictures I liked here too.

—Karen, grade 6

MAKE A TOWN

http://www.wolfenet.com/%7epor/foldup.html

With this free software download you can build your own town! Detailed instructions tell you how to download the software, then how to open up the program in order to make the town. You'll have to print out the buildings, cut them out, color them in, then fold them to put the town together.

I used this site to make a model town for a school project. It was really fun—and I got an A!

—Laura, grade 6

CALViN CooLBEE'S SPELLiNG ARCADE

http://www.coolbee.com

Challenge your spelling skills against these goofy-looking cartoon bees. You can get a preview of the games by clicking Calvin CoolBee's Spelling Arcade. You'll see three choices of spelling games, all of which make spelling an adventure—believe it or not! Download the free trial version for yourself!

I'm not great at spelling, but this game was fun. The spelling game where you have to collect the treasure was especially cool!

—Richard, grade 6

HYPERVISUAL BLOCKWORKS

http://hypervisual.com/blockworks/index.html

Very high tech, very futuristic looking, this site is awesome! The free download is all about building really interesting pictures by stacking colored blocks. But the blocks aren't like kindergarten-kiddie blocks. They're like metal, robotic-looking things. You have to see it for yourself! This site has won lots of awards. Take a look to find out why!

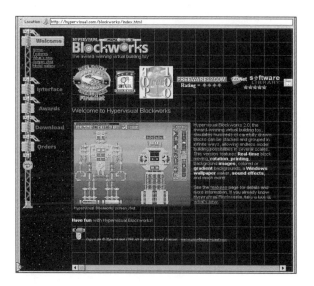

The things you can make here are really incredible. I printed them out to make posters for my wall.

—Davis, grade 7

iNTERNATioNAL KiDS' SPACE

http://www.kids-space.org/air/air.html

Look—and listen!—at this site. This is where you can download free music! Choose from Cool Compositions, Inspiring Instruments, and Soothing Songs. What's really neat about these tunes is that they were all composed by kids! And you can add your own musical compositions too! (The web page will tell you how.)

This site was a little young-looking, but I thought some of the music was really great!

—Jane, grade 6

GAME ZONE

These games are different from the games in the last chapter because, well, you don't have to download them! You can simply play them right on-line!

HEADBONE ZONE

http://www.headbone.com

When you're on-line, this is the place to be! There are so many games and other free things to do here—like Revenge of the Lunar Fringe and Iz and Auggie and the Invention Snatchers. You won't know where to start! Just choose a game to play, then go for it. You might even win a prize!

My favorite game is Mystery on Mars. You go to Mars, but you have to buy food and gas along the way.

—Patrick, grade 8

NATiONAL WiLDLiFE FUND

http://www.nwf.org/nwf/kids/index.html

When you think of the National Wildlife Fund, you probably imagine saving animals and learning about, well, wildlife. There *is* information about wildlife preservation here, but there's a lot more too. Of course there are free on-line games, like Mix 'Em and Match 'Em. But you can also take free virtual tours to learn about wetlands, endangered species, and water.

The free Madlibz game is my favorite part. I filled in words, then I read back a funny nature story I helped to write.

—Caitlin, grade 6

GiRL TECH

http://www.girltech.com

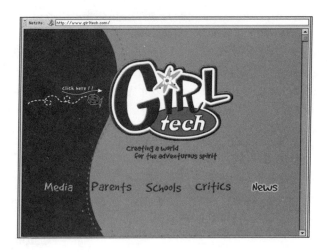

Sorry, guys! This site is really just for girls. You'll find lots of free games in the Game Café. The Crazy Story Maker lets you choose your own words to write a silly story. Also check out the Bow-tique.

I like that this site is just for girls. The Girl Views section is my favorite part.

—Janet, grade 7

KELLOGG'S CLUBHOUSE

http://www.kelloggs.com/club/games/index.html

Overdose on cereal here! Kellogg's, the people who bring you lots of breakfast stuff, has a fun web site. Drop by the Kellogg's Clubhouse and you'll find your choice of games, like Trivia Trail; Rock, Razzle, 'n' Roll; Cybersnackers; and Quest for the Golden Cereal Bowl.

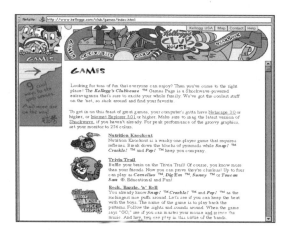

These games are so much fun. This site rules!

—Marcia, grade 7

ADVENTURE ON THE WEB

http://www-tjw.stanford.edu/adventure

Try this great game. You click the way to go, then watch your adventure unfold to explore a dungeon and its surroundings. You don't need to download anything—you simply click the direction buttons on the computer screen, then read to see where you've ended up. If you like fantasy adventure stories, this site is for you!

This is a great game because you control what happens. It takes a little bit of experimenting to figure it out, but the page has instructions and links that give you advice.

—Garret, grade 9

SNAPPLE

http://www.snapple.com

Snapple has a cool web site, complete with games. Click The Taste Is Worth the Hunt. You'll find a challenging word search and a hidden-picture puzzle, where you have to find the Snapple bottles.

KiDS' COLISEUM

http://www.nabiscokids.com/coliseum/co_index.html

Try your game-playing skills with these free games—Oreo Dunking Machine, Chips Ahoy! Chipulator, Time Surf, and Wild Side. These games are completely interactive, really colorful, and high quality. You don't want to miss them!

I think these games are a blast. I like Time Surf because it's science fictiony. It's a "showdown in space"!

—Alicia, grade 7

CHEF BOYARDEE ON-LINE ARCADE

http://www.chefboy.com/arcade/index.htm

Holy ravioli! Chef Boyardee, the company that brings us SpaghettiOs, has a game arcade with free games! Feed the Need and Ravioli Run are awesome interactive games. But you can also make your own Chef Boyardee commercial and put together your own comics, all for free! So dig in!

I loved Feed the Need. You help Beefy Boy, this kid on a skateboard, then a snowboard, maneuver through all sorts of dangers, including SUDD—Subterranean Uncontrollable Dastardly Demon. This game is excellent!
—Rodney, grade 8

FUNBRAIN.COM

http://www.funbrain.com

You'll find over a dozen free games at this incredible site, all of which help you with school stuff. Click your level, then play the free games to see how much you know. The games, like Fresh Baked Fractions, Word Detective, and Grammar Gorillas, are a great way to practice and improve school skills, all for free!

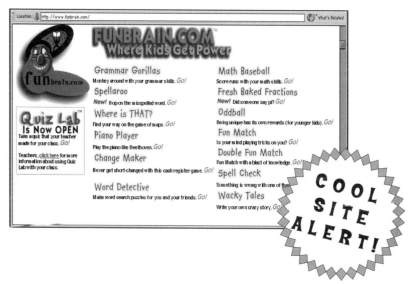

I found the free games at this site to be really helpful for school. One of my favorite games was Change Maker because it deals with something we have to do in the real world—figure out money and change.

—Alex, grade 7

CRAFT JAM

Whether it's a rainy day, or someone's birthday, or you're just bored, check out these sites. They're loaded with free instructions for fun stuff you can make, like cards, posters, and other arts-and-crafts ideas.

CRAYOLA

http://www.crayola.com

If you like to do arts and crafts, you should stop here first! Click on Craft Central to find the latest free craft idea or to stroll through the craft library. There are so many craft projects, we can't even list them all—we'd run out of room! Or if you'd rather just color in some pictures, stop by the Coloring Book. You'll also find games in the Game Room and stories in Story Time. And if you really want to know about Crayola, click on Inside Crayola. This site is perfect if you're looking for something to do!

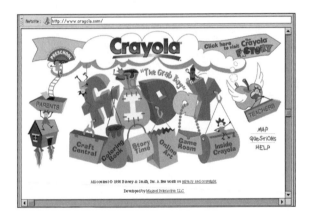

What I like about this site is that every week there's a new project. The first time I visited, they gave you free instructions for how to make an invisible, hidden picture. It was really cool!

—Carson, grade 6

GiNMeeTecH

http://www.webcom.com/gmt

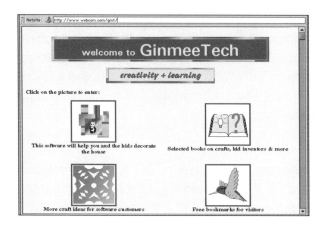

As this page tells you when you enter, it's all about "creativity and learning." There are books and software for sale here, but you can also find free bookmarks, fun animal facts, and even instructions for building paper airplanes.

The paper airplanes are the best. The directions tell you how to make these excellent Star Fighter and X Fighter planes.

—Paul, grade 6

MAKING FRIENDS

http://www.makingfriends.com

Do you want to give someone a special friendship bracelet or a beaded pendant you've made yourself? Then you can't miss this web page! It's full of many great—free!—ideas and patterns for making jewelry. You'll also find instructions for holiday crafts. At first the site may seem a bit young, but the ideas and patterns are excellent!

There was this nice daisy bracelet. The directions were easy to follow. After I printed out the free directions, I just had to get the beads and the string. I made one for myself and one for my best friend.

—Tamara, grade 7

WENDY'S WORLD OF CRAFTS

http://www.netfix.com/poptart/master.htm

Are you looking for that perfect ghoul to spruce up your window during Halloween? Or how about the perfect celebrate-summer decoration? Then stop by this site, where you'll find lots of fun craft projects for all the seasons and holidays throughout the year! You'll also find awesome recipes, like frosting paint and oatmeal clay, that you can make anytime!

I used the recipe for the edible necklaces to make party favors for all my friends. This is one of my favorite sites!

—Mariah, grade 6

MAGIC TRICKS

http://conjuror.com/magictricks

Want to learn some magic tricks—for free? Pop on over to this site. These simple instructions and pictures tell you how to stump your friends with traditional magic tricks, like The Self-Tying Handkerchief, The Mysterious Coin Balance, and Eleven Fingers. You'll also find links to other magic sites.

I tried these tricks on some of my friends, and they really worked. I like this site because it's fun to learn the secrets behind these magic tricks.
—Kelvin, grade 8

THE KID'S CHANNEL

http://members.tripod.com/~kid_channel/index.htm

At this site you'll find free coloring pages of animals and holiday stuff to print out. Click the picture you want to make it bigger before you print. Then click the Home button at the bottom of the web page to see what else this site has to offer, like the cartoon of the month, free games, jokes, stories, and recipes.

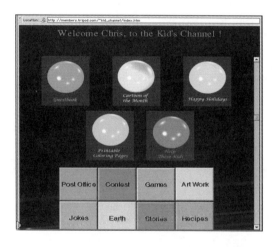

I thought the recipe section was the best! There were instructions for making a bird feeder, party hats, sidewalk art, and lots of other stuff.
—Wanda, grade 6

COLORING.COM

http://www.coloring.com/choose.html

This web site has great pictures that you can color right on-line. And you can even E-mail them! You can also print them out for free and then color them. Use the pictures for school projects, posters, cards, or anything else you feel like making! The pictures are really unique too. There aren't many craft web sites that have art of unicorns, leprechauns, and "ferret astaire"! Excellent pictures to add to your craft collection!

These pictures really ARE fun! In the fall they had a football theme. The running back was a rhinoceros in football gear. Hilarious! I used the pictures to decorate invitations for my family's Super Bowl party!

—Cliff, grade 7

EMMETT SCOTT'S ARTS & ACTIVITIES

http://www.cartooncorner.com/artspage.html

Want to learn how to draw cartoons? Check out the free instructions at this site. The step-by-step directions show you how to make cartoons come to life. You can also get drawing hints and the inside scoop on the types of jobs cartoonists have.

The artist gives us "secrets" for how to draw faces. It was pretty easy once I knew what to do. I like the cartoons I can draw now.

—Gary, grade 9

DiSNEY'S FAMiLY

http://www.family.disney.com/Categories/Activities

Choose a topic, choose your age, then click Go to find a gazillion arts-and-crafts ideas. You'll see projects for just about everything—paper crafts, candle making, clay, felt boards, and pipe-cleaner and Popsicle-stick art—all sorts of stuff to do, and all free! Check it out!

I scrolled through the project list and found some good ideas. I especially liked the sand painting. The directions are really for parents to do with kids, but kids can follow the directions too.

—Michelle, grade 6

BUBBLE MAKERS

http://www.bubbles.org/html/tools.htm

Think bubbles are cool? Then visit this site to learn different ways to make bubble blowers. You'll see how to construct bubble tools from simple things around the house, like hangers and cans.

I thought bubbles were just for little kids. But this site reminded me how much fun they are!

—Chris, grade 6

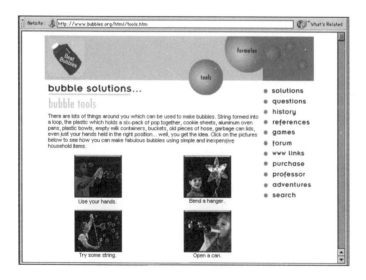

RADICAL READS

Many publishing companies have web sites for kids that include free bookmarks, games, and other cool stuff. You can even read magazines on-line! Flip through some of these.

SCHOLASTIC KIDS

http://www.scholastic.com/kids

You probably know lots of Scholastic books, like Animorphs, Goosebumps, The Baby-Sitters Club, and The Magic School Bus. You'll find lots of free related downloads for games, screen savers, and minimovies, plus special promotions, and sometimes even give-aways. (The promotions change from time to time, so you'll have to check every so often.)

There's always lots to do at this site. I like that you can read previews of new books that aren't in the stores yet.

—Jake, grade 7

PENGUIN PUTNAM YOUNG READERS

http://www.penguinputnam.com/yreaders/index.htm

Click Toy Box for the freebies. Be sure to check out the project ideas in the Creativity Corner, send cyberpostcards, color pages with interesting designs and excellent detailed pictures, and more. The mazes get an extra thumbs-up.

I like all the stuff you can make. And the coloring page of the castle was cool. I used it to illustrate a story I wrote for school.

—Jared, grade 5

SiMON SAYS KiDS.COM

http://www.simonsays.com/kids

This is a great place to learn about the latest children's books published by Simon & Schuster. Click on the book or topic you want. You can read about authors and books and even sign up for upcoming contests and sweepstakes, where you could win stuff! And click Cool Stuff to find free games!

STORYFUN!

http://www.mit.edu/storyfun

Check out this site to complete a free do-it-yourself story. The stories are pretty goofy—and they get even more goofy when you add your own silly words!

WiLLiAM MoRRoW BooKS

http://www.williammorrow.com/wm/children.html

This site is a bit serious, but if you like books and reading, you're in the right place. You'll find previews of upcoming books and you can send free postcards to your friends, but best of all, you can make bookmarks! Click on the bookmark you want, print it out, and there you go! Of course, you can color them. Or print out two bookmarks and glue them back to back. (This will give you pictures on both sides of the bookmark, not to mention making the bookmark sturdier!)

The bookmarks are big and colorful. I poked a hole in the top of mine and added some yarn too.

—Amie, grade 6

HARPERCOLLiNS CHiLDREN'S BOOKS

http://www.harperchildrens.com

COOL SITE ALERT!

Drop by HarperCollins' Big Busy House for fun book-related things to do. If you click into Games, you can make your own creature in Switcheroos (animals, aliens, robots, vehicles) for free. In Wacky Words you give the words to make your own silly story. There's even a Quote Quiz. And, of course, you can read stuff about new books.

I love Switcheroos. You can make some awesome-looking creatures, then print them out for free and use them for puppets.

—Carla, grade 6

JOSIE'S CLUBHOUSE

http://www.jitterbug.com/pages/josie.html

You never know—books on the web might be the wave of the future! Catch the wave here by reading this book on-line—for free! You could even print out the chapters to make reading the book easier. Before you start, read the profiles of the characters. Then click the chapters to begin.

I've never read a book on the computer before. It was fun! I like Josie. I thought she was a good character.

—Melissa, grade 5

CYBERKIDS

http://www.cyberkids.com

This is a free on-line magazine with tons of stuff to do. Check out the Reading Room, the Gallery, the Shockwave Movie in the Theater, and the Contest Zone. And what site would be complete without games? Plus, there is a link to *Cyberteens,* an on-line magazine for older kids.

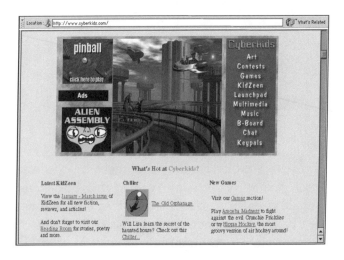

I liked reading the adventure story. Every week a new part was added.
—Warren, grade 5

MiDLiNK MAGAZiNE

http://www2.ncsu.edu/unity/lockers/
project/midlinknc/vy/index.local.html

Here's another free on-line magazine for you to check out. It's for kids in the middle grades or, as they describe it, "generally ages 10 to 15." The magazine is filled with stories and articles that other kids have written. It really is a link between you and kids in middle schools all over the world.

The stories are interesting. It's fun to see what people in other schools are doing and thinking.

—Erica, grade 8

SPORTS ILLUSTRATED FOR KIDS

http://www.sikids.com

Want to see what *Sports Illustrated for Kids* is all about? Check out this web site! Besides articles on sports, you can try the trivia challenge and tile puzzle, view funny photos, and state your own opinions, all for free. Plus, sign up to get a free trial issue of the "real" *Sports Illustrated for Kids.*

The on-line magazine is a good way to get quick information about sports. The articles are up-to-date and interesting.

—Jackie, grade 7

NATIONAL GEOGRAPHIC WORLD MAGAZINE

http://www.nationalgeographic.com/media/world/index.html

Want to see what's in the latest issue of *National Geographic World* magazine? Check out its official web site. You'll be able to read the main article—complete with color pictures for free. You can even suggest ideas for stories.

I've always loved this magazine, so I was really happy when I found the web site.

—Paul, grade 7

TiME FOR KiDS

http://www.pathfinder.com/TFK

Keep up-to-date about the world with this free on-line magazine. Look at the cartoons, exchange ideas with other kids, and learn what's happening in our world. A fun way to check out what's up, this magazine is a kids' version of the adult news magazine *Time*.

I like the stories and pictures. You can answer surveys and state your opinions, right there!

—Justine, grade 8

PC GAMES MAGAZINE

http://www.games.net/pcgames/resources/sub.html

If you're into CD-ROM games, then check out the site for this computer-games magazine. Sign up to receive not only two free issues of *PC Games* magazine but to get two free CD-ROMs that have game samples. Remember to ask your parents before you sign up for this "trial" subscription.

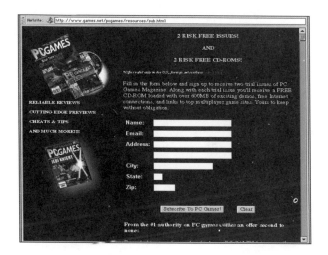

PC GAMER ON-LINE

http://service.imaginemedia.com/group/gppg/8C6X.html

Not to be confused with the above publication, this is *PC Gamer* magazine. See the difference? Fill out the form for a "trial" subscription (one free issue). Remember to ask your parents first.

MAiL MADNESS

Do you like getting stuff in the mail? How about getting stuff in the mail for free? Visit these sites to get food, stickers, even a tree—for free! You'll have to give your name and address, so make sure it's okay with your parents.

JELLY BELLY CANDY SHOP

http://www.jellybelly.com

What could be better than getting free jelly beans in the mail? All you have to do is take a quick survey. You can also read the history of the jelly bean, take a factory tour, see jelly bean art, and more! You can even join the Jelly Belly Taste Bud Club!

I like the free Jelly Belly recipe. It tells you which jelly beans to mix to get a new flavor!

—Carrie, grade 7

CHiPS AHOY!

http://www.chipsahoy.com/

Visit this site and you may find out how to get a free glow-in-the-dark T-shirt. All you have to do is count all the chips you see on the web site. As they say, "Every chip counts." This is a fun site all around, with a game room and a cookie museum.

This is one of my favorite sites. The cookie museum rules! You see goofy paintings of famous scenes, like the Mona Lisa eating cookies (that's why she's smiling!) and Napoleon Cookie Monster hiding cookies in his shirt.
—Kelly, grade 6

ARBoR DAY

http://www.arborday.net/kids

Did you know that the largest living thing on our planet is a tree? Arbor Day is all about appreciating trees. At this site you'll not only find coloring pages, but you'll find out how to get your own tree—free! Print out the coupon and mail it in for your free tree. (You'll have to pay for postage.)

I like this site because I love trees and plants. This site tells us why trees are important to the environment.

—Marcus, grade 6

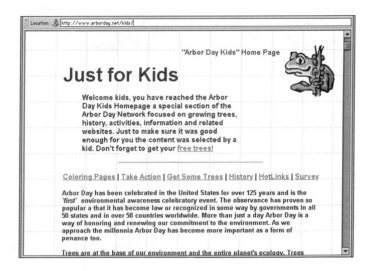

THE KIDS SHOPPER

http://www.thekidsshopper.com

This site has lots of catalogs to send away for, clubs to join, and contests to enter. But most important, if you send them a self-addressed, stamped envelope with a 55-cent stamp on it, they'll send you a free grab bag of "goodies and toys," as they describe it. You never know!

What's really cool about this site is that there's always an update of things you can get for free. And you can still check out old lists of stuff in case you missed any. It's like a shopping list for kids on the web!

—Melissa, grade 6

CREATiVE WONDERS CDS

http://www.cwonders.com/forms/testform.html

This is an amazing opportunity! How would you like to get free CD-ROMs just because you told a company what you thought about it? Pretty cool, right? All you have to do is sign up to be a CD-ROM tester! The site tells you what to do. Give those CD-ROM makers your input!

GREEN MOUNTAiN BLOCKS

http://www.virtualvermont.com/gmblocks/index.html

Get some free building blocks! They're strong, sturdy, wooden blocks, perfect for school projects or to build stuff at home. If you'd like a sample, click View Our Catalog. Read the Please Note, which explains that the sample is free, plus $2.00 for shipping and handling. View their products, or click Order Form. Print it out, fill it out, and mail it in!

STAR TREK CARDS

http://www.atlaseditions.com/scripts/salesform.pl?
HDFX:901366540.205.188.192.31&trekuniverse1/forms.html

If you're into *Star Trek,* then you'll want these 30 "official *Star Trek* cards"—free (if you don't count 99 cents for shipping and handling)! You must be eighteen years old to get the cards, so ask your parents to help you.

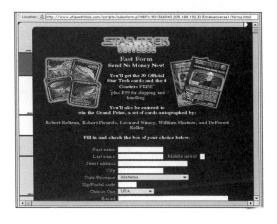

I had my parents order these cards for me because I love Star Trek. The cards are the greatest!

—Dan, grade 8

AVERY KiDS FUNHOUSE

http://www.avery.com/kids/samples.html

Check out this site for up-to-date info on giveaway samples. The Avery Kids Sample Pack changes, but in the month we were on, they were giving out free stickers and greeting cards. And while you're there, you should also stop by the Avery Kids Arcade for free games!

I can't wait to get my free sample! The games in the arcade are fun, like Make-a-Face and the puzzle game.

—Catrina, grade 6

CATALOG REQUEST CENTER

http://www.smartshop1.com/crc

At this site you'll find out how to get free catalogs for just about anything. Click on the topic you want, like gifts, music and videos, or hobbies and crafts, to name a few.

I'm really into collecting stuff, and there's a section of catalogs that feature collectibles, like sports stuff or stamps. It's a great resource!
                                                            —Leslie, grade 7

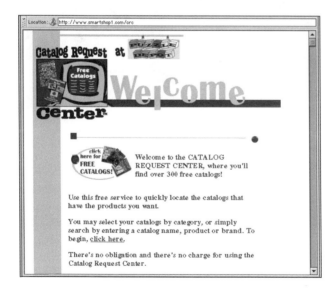

SKATERS HAVEN

http://www.skaters-haven.com

At this site, you can sign on to their mailing list and get a free decal.
To get there, click Free Stuff on the home page.

If you're into skateboarding, check this out!

—Ryan, grade 6

GLOSSARY

browser   a program that lets you go to specific addresses on the web and display web sites

chat   to talk with others on the Internet

download   to move a file from the Internet onto your desktop

E-mail   "electronic" mail; these are the notes you read and send over the Internet

E-mail address   a personal address you use to send and receive electronic mail over the computer; it's just like the real address you use to mail a letter to someone's home

home   usually the main page of a web site

link   on a web page, this is a picture or underlined word or words; when you click them, you move to another location, on the same or even a different web site

search engine   a service that helps you find addresses of sites on the web

web   the World Wide Web

web address   what you type in after http:// that takes you to a web page

WEB SITE INDEX

GinmeeTech . . . . http://www.webcom.com/gmt

Girl Tech . . . . http://www.girltech.com

Green Mountain Blocks . . . . http://www.virtualvermont.com/
gmblocks/index.html

GusTown . . . . http://www.gustown.com/home/gustownsummer.html

HarperCollins Children's Books . . . . http://www.harperchildrens.com

Headbone Zone . . . . http://www.headbone.com

Horsefun . . . . http://www.horsefun.com

Hypervisual Blockworks . . . . . . http://hypervisual.com/blockworks/index.html

International Kids' Space . . . . http://www.kids-space.org/air/air.html

The Irwin Fun Factory . . . . http://www.irwin-toy.com

Jelly Belly Candy Shop . . . . http://www.jellybelly.com

Josie's Clubhouse . . . . http://www.jitterbug.com/pages/josie.html

Kellogg's Clubhouse . . . . http://www.kelloggs.com/club/games/index.html

The Kid's Channel . . . . . . http://members.tripod.com/~kid_channel/index.htm

Kids' Coliseum . . . . http://www.nabiscokids.com/coliseum/co_index.html

Kids Domain . . . . http://www.kidsdomain.com

The Kids Shopper . . . . http://www.thekidsshopper.com

Magic Tricks . . . . http://conjuror.com/magictricks

Make a Town http://www.wolfenet.com/%7epor/foldup.html

Making Friends . . . . http://www.makingfriends.com

Microsoft Kids! . . . . http://www.microsoft.com/kids/freestuff

MidLink Magazine http://www2.ncsu.edu/unity/lockers/project/
midlinknc/vy/index.local.html

National Geographic World Magazine . . . . . . http://www.nationalgeographic.com/
media/world/index.html